Intro to
Italian

Bela Davis

Italiano

Abdo Kids Junior
is an Imprint of Abdo Kids
abdobooks.com

Abdo
INTRO TO LANGUAGE
Kids

abdobooks.com

Published by Abdo Kids, a division of ABDO, P.O. Box 398166, Minneapolis, Minnesota 55439.
Copyright © 2024 by Abdo Consulting Group, Inc. International copyrights reserved in all countries.
No part of this book may be reproduced in any form without written permission from the publisher.
Abdo Kids Junior™ is a trademark and logo of Abdo Kids.

Printed in the United States of America, North Mankato, Minnesota.

102023

012024

THIS BOOK CONTAINS
RECYCLED MATERIALS

Consultant: Francesca Rossi

Photo Credits: Getty Images, Shutterstock

Production Contributors: Teddy Borth, Jennie Forsberg, Grace Hansen

Design Contributors: Candice Keimig, Colleen McLaren

Library of Congress Control Number: 2023937676

Publisher's Cataloging-in-Publication Data

Names: Davis, Bela, author.

Title: Intro to Italian / by Bela Davis

Description: Minneapolis, Minnesota : Abdo Kids, 2024 | Series: Intro to language | Includes online
    resources and index.

Identifiers: ISBN 9781098268312 (lib. bdg.) | ISBN 9781098269012 (ebook) | ISBN 9781098269364
    (Read-to-Me ebook)

Subjects: LCSH: Italian language--Juvenile literature. | Informal language learning--Juvenile literature. |
    Language and languages--Juvenile literature. | Bilingual books--Juvenile literature.

Classification: DDC 418.00--dc23

Table of Contents

Intro to Italian

Italian is spoken around the world. Let's learn some words!

Italian	**benvenuto**
(sound guide)	(ben·venu·to)
English	welcome

Europe

Italy

Africa

uno
(oo•noh)

one

due
(doo•eh)

two

sei
(seh•e)

six

sette
(seht•teh)

seven

tre
(treh)

three

quattro
(kwah•troh)

four

cinque
(chin•kweh)

five

otto
(oh•toh)

eight

nove
(noh•veh)

nine

dieci
(dee•eh•chee)

ten

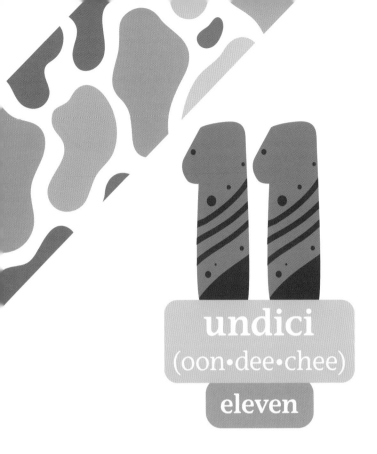

undici
(oon•dee•chee)

eleven

dodici
(doh•dee•chee)

twelve

sedici
(seh•dee•chee)

sixteen

diciassette
(dee•cha•set•teh)

seventeen

tredici
(treh•dee•chee)

thirteen

quattordici
(kwah•tor•dee•chee)

fourteen

quindici
(kween•dee•chee)

fifteen

diciotto
(dee•chee•oh•toh)

eighteen

diciannove
(dee•chahn•noh•veh)

nineteen

venti
(ven•tee)

twenty

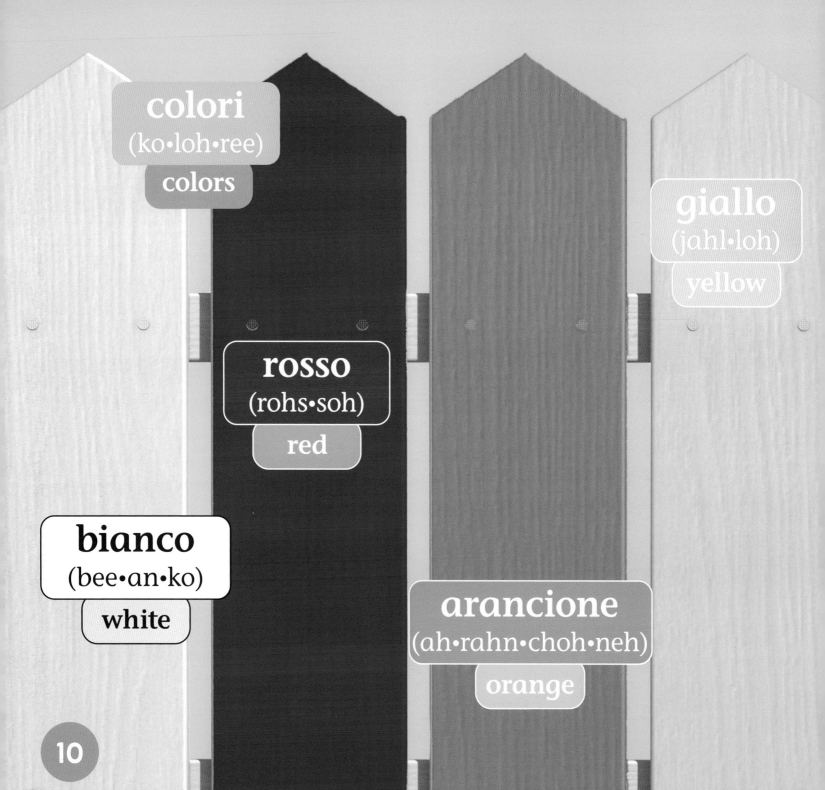

colori
(ko•loh•ree)
colors

rosso
(rohs•soh)
red

giallo
(jahl•loh)
yellow

bianco
(bee•an•ko)
white

arancione
(ah•rahn•choh•neh)
orange

10

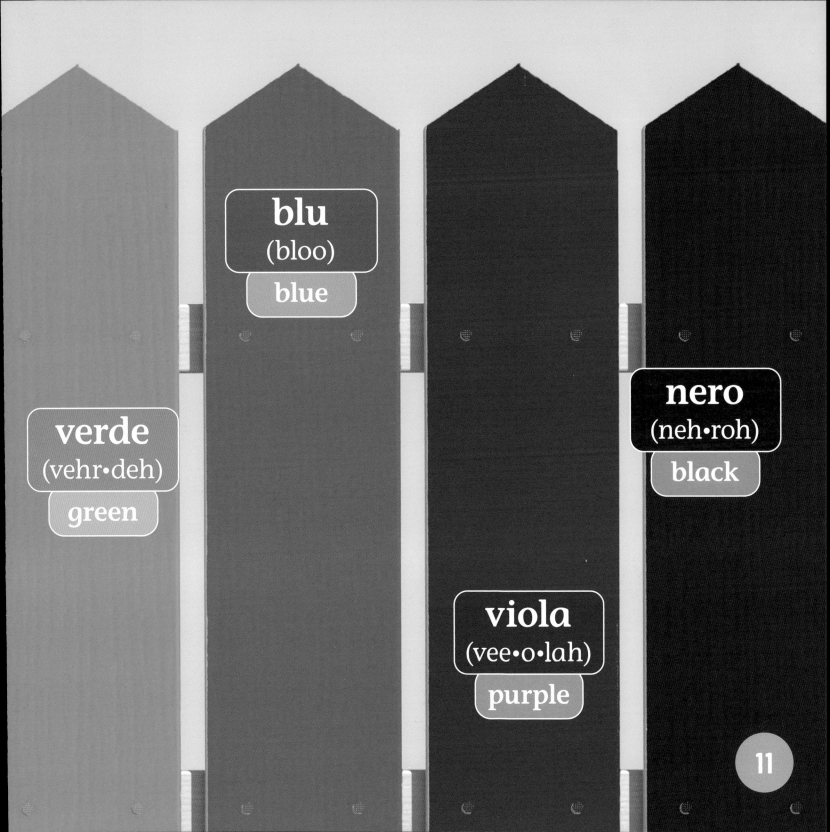

verde
(vehr•deh)
green

blu
(bloo)
blue

viola
(vee•o•lah)
purple

nero
(neh•roh)
black

11

ciao
(chow)

hello

arrivederci
(ah•ree•veh•dehr•chee)

goodbye

buongiorno
(bwohn•jor•no)

good morning

buona notte
(bwohn•nah•no•teh)

good night

per favore
(pehr fah•voh•reh)

please

grazie
(grah•tsy•eh)

thank you

sì
(see)

yes

no
(noh)

no

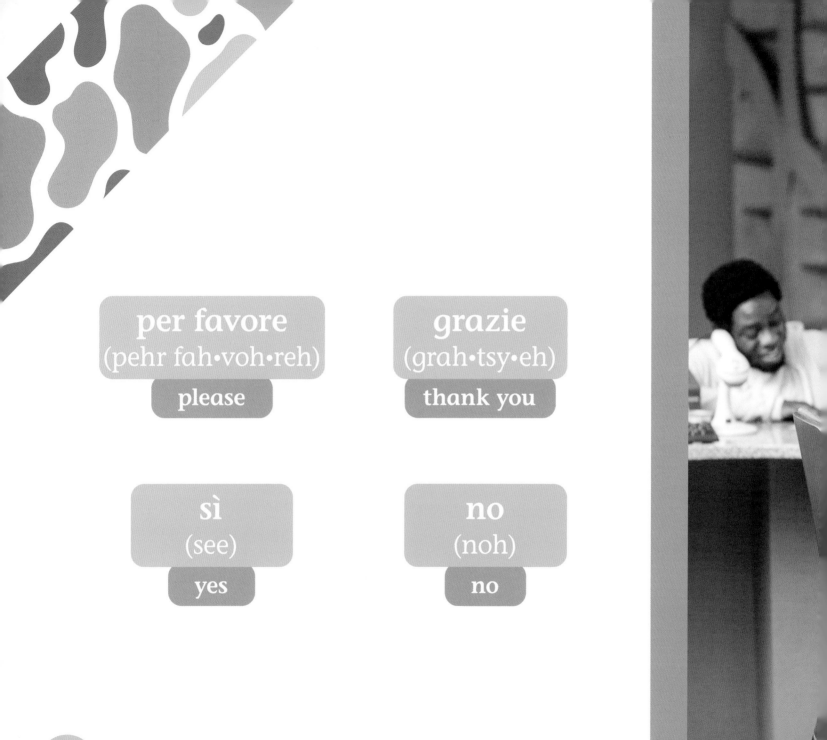

la famiglia
(fa•meel•ya)
the family

la mamma
(mam•ma)
mom

il papà
(pa•pa)
dad

la sorella
(so•rel•la)
sister

il fratello
(fra•tel•lo)
brother

la nonna
(nohn•na)

grandma

il nonno
(nohn•no)

grandpa

la zia
(zee•ah)

aunt

lo zio
(zee•oh)

uncle

gli animali
(ah•nee•mah•lee)
the animals

il gatto
(gaht•toh)
cat

il cane
(ka•ne)
dog

20

l'uccello
(oo•chel•loh)
bird

il pesce
(peh•sheh)
fish

21

Luoghi – Places

la casa
(ka•za)

house

la scuola
(skwo•la)

school

il parco
(pahr•ko)

park

la spiaggia
(spee•ah•ja)

beach

L'alfabeto – The Alphabet

letter	sound
A	ah
B	bee
C	chee
D	dee
E	eh
F	eh•ffeh
G	jee
H	ah•kkah
I	ee
L	eh•lleh
M	eh•mmeh
N	eh•nneh
O	oh
P	pee
Q	koo
R	eh•rreh
S	eh•sseh
T	tee
U	oo
V	vee/voo
Z	dzeh•tah

Index

Abdo Kids
ONLINE
FREE! ONLINE MULTIMEDIA RESOURCES

Visit **abdokids.com**
to access crafts, games,
videos, and more!

Use Abdo Kids code

IIK8312

or scan this QR code!

24